CHECKERBOARD BIOGRAPHY LIBRARY

U.S. PRESIDENTS

The
United States Presidents

RICHARD NIXON

ABDO Publishing Company

Tamara L. Britton

visit us at
www.abdopublishing.com

Published by ABDO Publishing Company, 8000 West 78th Street, Edina, Minnesota 55439.
Copyright © 2009 by Abdo Consulting Group, Inc. International copyrights reserved in all
countries. No part of this book may be reproduced in any form without written permission from the
publisher. The Checkerboard Library™ is a trademark and logo of ABDO Publishing Company.

Printed in the United States of America, North Mankato, Minnesota.
012009 042013

Cover Photo: Getty Images
Interior Photos: AP Images pp. 10, 13, 16, 19, 20, 21, 22, 27, 29; Corbis pp. 5, 9, 12, 14, 15;
    iStockphoto pp. 25, 32; National Archives p. 26

Editor: Megan M. Gunderson
Art Direction & Cover Design: Neil Klinepier
Interior Design: Jaime Martens

Library of Congress Cataloging-in-Publication Data

Britton, Tamara L., 1963-
  Richard Nixon / Tamara L. Britton.
    p. cm. -- (The United States presidents)
  Includes index.
  ISBN 978-1-60453-468-9
  1. Nixon, Richard M. (Richard Milhous), 1913-1994--Juvenile literature. 2. Presidents--United
States--Biography--Juvenile literature. I. Title.

  E856.B73 2009
  973.924092--dc22
  [B]
                              2008033506

CONTENTS

RICHARD NIXON

In 1969, Richard Nixon became the thirty-seventh president of the United States. It was a great achievement. Nixon had come from a poor family. He had worked hard to improve himself and to earn success.

As a young boy, Nixon worked in his father's business. In school, he did well and won a college **scholarship**. Then, Nixon went to law school and became a lawyer.

In 1946, Nixon was elected to the U.S. House of Representatives. Five years later, he entered the U.S. Senate as its youngest member. He was just 38 years old. Then in 1953, Nixon became the second-youngest vice president in U.S. history.

In 1968, Nixon was elected president. As president, he worked with other countries toward world peace. Nixon also passed laws to improve life for Americans. In 1972, he easily won reelection.

However, Nixon made some bad decisions during his first term. They overshadowed the good he had done. As a result, Nixon became the first president in U.S. history to resign from office.

TIMELINE

1913 - On January 9, Richard Milhous Nixon was born in Yorba Linda, California.

1940 - On June 21, Nixon married Thelma Catherine Patricia "Pat" Ryan.

1946 - Nixon's first daughter, Patricia, was born on February 21; Nixon defeated Horace "Jerry" Voorhis on November 5 to win a seat in the U.S. House of Representatives.

1948 - Nixon's second daughter, Julie, was born on July 5.

1950 - On November 7, Nixon defeated Helen Douglas to become a U.S. senator.

1952 - On September 23, Nixon gave the Checkers speech; Nixon was elected vice president under Dwight D. Eisenhower on November 4.

1960 - Nixon lost the presidential election to John F. Kennedy on November 8.

1968 - On November 5, Nixon defeated Hubert H. Humphrey to become president of the United States.

1969 - On January 20, Nixon became the thirty-seventh U.S. president.

1972 - Burglars broke into the Democratic National Committee office at the Watergate Hotel on June 17; Nixon was reelected on November 7.

1973 - Vice President Spiro T. Agnew resigned on October 10; Nixon appointed Gerald Ford vice president.

1974 - Nixon resigned on August 9; Vice President Ford became president.

1993 - Pat Nixon died on June 22.

1994 - Richard Nixon died on April 22 from complications of a stroke.

DID YOU KNOW?

Richard Nixon's brother Francis was named after their father. He and his brothers Harold, Arthur, and Edward were named after kings of England.

While a student at Duke Law School, Nixon did not have much money. So, every day for breakfast he ate a candy bar. The bars cost only five cents. But Nixon ended up paying much more for those meals. His dentist had to fix the damage all that candy did to his teeth!

The 1960 presidential election was not the first time Richard Nixon and John F. Kennedy debated. On April 21, 1947, the two freshmen congressmen debated the Taft-Hartley Act in McKeesport, Pennsylvania.

PRESIDENT OF THE
POTUS
UNITED STATES

EARLY YEARS

Richard Milhous Nixon was born in Yorba Linda, California, on January 9, 1913. He was Francis and Hannah Nixon's second son. Richard had an older brother named Harold. His younger brothers were Francis, who was called Donald, Arthur, and Edward.

In 1922, the Nixons moved to Whittier, California. There, Francis opened a gas station and grocery store. Richard and his brothers worked in the store. Richard learned to serve people and to be polite. These lessons helped him later in life.

The Nixons were **Quakers**. Much of their family life centered on religion. They attended church services three times on Sunday and once on Wednesday.

Richard worked hard to improve himself. As a boy, he read newspapers and learned to **debate**. He also played the piano and the organ. In school,

FAST FACTS

BORN - January 9, 1913
WIFE - Thelma Catherine Patricia "Pat" Ryan (1912–1993)
CHILDREN - 2
POLITICAL PARTY - Republican
AGE AT INAUGURATION - 56
YEARS SERVED - 1969–1974
VICE PRESIDENTS - Spiro T. Agnew, Gerald Ford
DIED - April 22, 1994, age 81

Richard earned good grades and was skilled at **debate**.

The Nixons faced many challenges. Though they all worked in the store, it did not make much money. Then, Richard's brother Arthur died from **tuberculosis**. Soon, Richard's brother Harold also died of the disease. He and Richard had been very close.

After his brothers died, Richard worked even more. Every day, he got up at 4:00 AM to work in the store. He worked after school, too. Still, Richard graduated from high school near the top of his class.

Richard (far right) *and his family*

STUDENT LEADER

Richard's good grades earned him a **scholarship** at Harvard University in Cambridge, Massachusetts. But, his family could not afford to pay his living expenses. So, Richard could not accept the award. He was very disappointed.

In 1930, Richard entered Whittier College in Whittier, California. In his first year, Richard was elected class president. The next year, he was the star of the **debate** team. He won nearly all of his 50 debates!

At Whittier, Richard made the football team. He wasn't a great player. But he became better with practice.

One of Richard's favorite sports was football. On the Whittier College football team, he played on the offensive line.

10

He also appeared in school plays and musicals. In his senior year, Richard was elected student body president.

Richard did well in history, but he had trouble with math and science. With hard work, Richard soon did well in those subjects, too. In 1934, he graduated second in his class.

Once again, Richard's success earned him a **scholarship**. This time, he attended Duke University School of Law in Durham, North Carolina. To pay his living expenses, he worked in the college library.

At Duke, Richard was known for his leadership. Once again he was elected student body president. In his final year of law school, Richard became president of the Duke **Bar Association**. In June 1937, he graduated third in his class.

Richard wanted to stay on the East Coast. But he did not get any job offers there. So, he returned to Whittier and joined the law firm of Wingert and Bewley. Through more hard work, Richard soon became a **partner**. The firm became Wingert, Bewley, and Nixon.

FAMILY MAN

In Whittier, Nixon met Thelma Catherine Patricia Ryan. She went by the name Pat. Pat had grown up in California. Both of her parents had died before she was 17 years old.

Like Richard, Pat had also worked hard to be successful. She had worked at various jobs to pay for college. Pat graduated from the University of Southern California in 1937. Then, she taught high school. She and Nixon dated for two years. They were married on June 21, 1940.

World War II had started in 1939. In 1942, Nixon joined the U.S. Navy.

Until they got their marriage license, Nixon did not know Pat's real name!

He became an operations officer with the South Pacific Combat Air Transport Command. Nixon's success continued in the navy. He was promoted to lieutenant commander.

After the war ended, the Nixons moved to Baltimore, Maryland. There, Nixon worked for the navy while awaiting his release from duty. Then in September 1945, a Whittier political group asked Nixon to run for Congress. The offer changed his life forever.

Nixon joined the navy even though he suffered from seasickness.

The Nixons returned to Whittier to campaign. California voters liked Nixon. He spoke well and shared many of their views. On November 5, 1946, Nixon defeated Horace "Jerry" Voorhis. He won a seat in the U.S. House of Representatives.

During the campaign, the Nixons had their first child. Patricia, called Tricia, was born on February 21, 1946. Their second daughter, Julie, was born on July 5, 1948.

CONGRESSMAN

In Congress, Nixon quickly began working to serve the American people. He served on the committee that created the **Marshall Plan**. He also served on the House Education and Labor Committee. There, he helped write the **Taft-Hartley Act**.

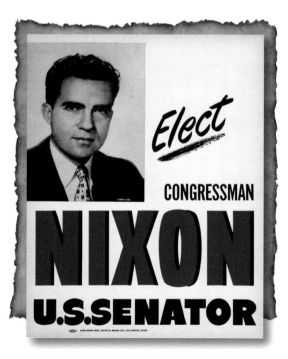

Nixon's most important work was on the House Committee on Un-American Activities. There, he worked on the Alger Hiss case. Hiss was a former government worker. He was accused of giving government papers to a Communist spy. Nixon's efforts helped convict Hiss of **perjury**. The case made Nixon famous.

Nixon then ran against Helen Douglas for a seat in the U.S. Senate. On November 7, 1950, Nixon easily won the election. He took office on January 3, 1951. At 38 years old, he was the youngest U.S. senator.

Eisenhower (left) *and Nixon on the campaign trail*

More success followed. In 1952, **Republicans** chose Nixon to run for vice president. Their presidential candidate was Dwight D. Eisenhower.

But a few days later, the *New York Post* newspaper printed a story about Nixon. It said that he took money and gifts from California businessmen in exchange for political favors. The public was shocked. Some Republicans wanted to remove Nixon as the vice presidential candidate.

Nixon holds Checkers. Nixon's televised speech became known as the Checkers speech.

On September 23, 1952, Nixon took his case directly to the American people. In a nationally televised speech, he claimed he had not misused any contributions. Nixon said the money paid for expenses he did not want taxpayers to pay. Nixon said he never used the money for himself. And, no one got political favors in return for money.

As for the gifts, someone in Texas had given Nixon a cocker spaniel. Tricia had named the dog Checkers. Nixon said, "And as you know, the kids, like all kids, love the dog, and I just want to say this right now, that regardless of what they say about it, we're going to keep it."

Nixon told Americans he did not want to quit running for vice president. But he said he would step down if they felt he should. Nixon asked them to write the **Republican National Committee** with their decision.

The speech was a success. Americans wanted Nixon to remain on the ticket. On November 4, 1952, Eisenhower and Nixon won the election. They easily defeated **Democratic** candidate Adlai E. Stevenson II and his **running mate**, John Sparkman.

VICE PRESIDENT

Nixon was an active vice president. He went to many **cabinet** meetings. Nixon traveled the world to make speeches for the United States. And, he took over presidential duties several times when Eisenhower had health problems. The president had a heart attack in 1955. He had an operation in 1956 and a **stroke** in 1957.

In 1960, the **Republican** Party chose Nixon as its candidate for president. His **running mate** was Henry Cabot Lodge Jr. They campaigned against **Democrat** John F. Kennedy and his running mate, Lyndon B. Johnson.

For the first time in history, the two presidential candidates **debated** on television. Nixon was an accomplished debater. But, he had been sick with the flu. And, he refused to wear any makeup. So, he did not look good. Kennedy was fit and tanned. He looked young and full of energy.

Between 60 and 70 million viewers watched Nixon and Kennedy on television. Their debates became known as The Great Debates.

Those who listened to the **debates** on the radio thought Nixon had won. But, those who watched the debates on television thought Kennedy had won.

On November 8, 1960, almost 69 million people went to the polls. Kennedy won by less than 120,000 **popular votes**! It was one of the closest elections in U.S. history. For the first time, Nixon had lost an election.

The 1960 presidential election had both the closest margin of victory and the highest voter turnout in the 1900s.

Nixon returned to California. Two years later, he ran for governor against **incumbent** Pat Brown. But, he lost the election. Nixon's work in politics seemed over.

After the election, Nixon met with newspaper reporters. He accused them of not telling the truth about him. Nixon said it was his last press conference.

The Nixons then moved to New York. There, Nixon worked as a lawyer. But already, he was thinking about his future in politics.

Nixon's "last press conference" at the Beverly Hilton Hotel in Los Angeles, California, lasted 15 minutes. He spoke the entire time and took no questions from reporters.

PRESIDENT NIXON

Nixon did not run for president in 1964. It was the first time in 12 years his name was not on the **ballot**. Instead, Nixon campaigned for **Republican** presidential nominee Barry Goldwater. Nixon traveled 50,000 miles (80,500 km) through 36 states! However, Goldwater lost the election.

Nixon continued to campaign for Republican politicians. In 1966, he traveled 30,000 miles (48,300 km) and visited 35 states. Nixon's hard work helped Republicans win many elections that year.

In 1968, Republicans picked Nixon to run for president. Nixon chose Maryland governor Spiro T. Agnew as his **running mate**.

Nixon worked day and night on his campaign. On November 5, 1968, Nixon defeated **Democrat** Hubert H. Humphrey and his running mate, Edmund Muskie. On January 20, 1969, Nixon was **inaugurated** president of the United States.

Nixon with Spiro T. Agnew (left)

PRESIDENT NIXON'S CABINET

FIRST TERM
JANUARY 20, 1969– JANUARY 20, 1973

- **STATE** – William P. Rogers
- **TREASURY** – David M. Kennedy,
  John B. Connally Jr. (from February 11, 1971)
  George P. Shultz (from June 12, 1972)
- **DEFENSE** – Melvin R. Laird
- **ATTORNEY GENERAL** – John N. Mitchell
  Richard G. Kleindienst (from June 12, 1972)
- **INTERIOR** – Walter J. Hickel
  Rogers C.B. Morton (from January 29, 1971)
- **AGRICULTURE** – Clifford M. Hardin
  Earl L. Butz (from December 2, 1971)
- **COMMERCE** – Maurice H. Stans
  Peter G. Peterson (from February 21, 1972)
- **LABOR** – George P. Shultz
  James D. Hodgson (from July 2, 1970)
- **HEALTH, EDUCATION, AND WELFARE** –
  Robert H. Finch
  Elliot L. Richardson (from June 24, 1970)
- **HOUSING AND URBAN DEVELOPMENT** –
  George W. Romney
- **TRANSPORTATION** – John A. Volpe

SECOND TERM
JANUARY 20, 1973– AUGUST 9, 1974

- **STATE** – William P. Rogers
  Henry A. Kissinger (from September 22, 1973)
- **TREASURY** – George P. Shultz
  William E. Simon (from May 8, 1974)
- **DEFENSE** – Elliot L. Richardson
  James R. Schlesinger (from July 2, 1973)
- **ATTORNEY GENERAL** – Richard G. Kleindienst
  Elliot L. Richardson (from May 25, 1973)
  William B. Saxbe (from January 4, 1974)
- **INTERIOR** – Rogers C.B. Morton
- **AGRICULTURE** – Earl L. Butz
- **COMMERCE** – Frederick B. Dent
- **LABOR** – Peter J. Brennan
- **HEALTH, EDUCATION, AND WELFARE** –
  Caspar W. Weinberger
- **HOUSING AND URBAN DEVELOPMENT** –
  James T. Lynn
- **TRANSPORTATION** – Claude S. Brinegar

PEACEMAKER

When Nixon became president, the United States was fighting in the **Vietnam War**. Also, the United States was involved in the **Cold War**. The **Six-Day War** had recently ended in the Middle East. In his **inaugural** speech, Nixon promised he would work for world peace.

To bring about peace, Nixon visited countries all over the world. He met with Communist leaders as well as the Pope. He also visited China to improve relations with that country. And, he became the first U.S. president to visit Moscow in the Soviet Union. There, Nixon signed a treaty that would slow the making of nuclear weapons.

In the United States, Nixon worked to cut government spending. He started wage and price controls to help lower **inflation**. This kept the cost of products such as food, clothing, gas, and houses from increasing.

SUPREME COURT APPOINTMENTS

WARREN E. BURGER - 1969

HARRY A. BLACKMUN - 1970

LEWIS F. POWELL JR. - 1972

WILLIAM H. REHNQUIST - 1972

24

More than 58,000 Americans died in the Vietnam War. Some served against their will because they were drafted. President Nixon negotiated a cease-fire effective January 28, 1973, and he ended the draft.

President Nixon also signed laws that created the **Environmental** Protection Agency, the National Oceanic and Atmospheric Administration, and the Occupational Safety and Health Administration.

Americans were happy with Nixon's work. On November 7, 1972, he and Vice President Agnew ran for reelection. Their opponents were **Democrats** George McGovern and R. Sargent Shriver. Nixon was one of the nation's most popular presidents. He easily won reelection.

A TRAGIC ENDING

Despite Nixon's popularity, a **scandal** soon overshadowed his success. On June 17, 1972, burglars had been caught breaking into the **Democratic National Committee**'s main office. The office was in the Watergate Hotel building in Washington, D.C. Some **Republicans** had hired the burglars to steal information to help Nixon's reelection campaign.

Nixon also faced other troubles. Vice President Agnew was accused of accepting bribes. He was forced to resign on October 10, 1973. Nixon then appointed Gerald Ford as vice president.

Throughout the problems with the vice presidency, the Watergate scandal grew. Nixon knew about the break-in. He had tried to cover it up. Congress wanted to **impeach** Nixon for his actions.

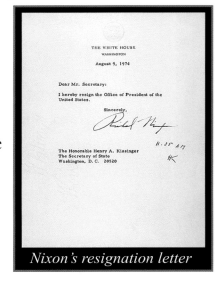

Nixon's resignation letter

Nixon resigned on August 9, 1974, before he could be impeached. It was the first time a U.S. president had quit. Vice President Ford became president.

On September 8, 1974, President Ford pardoned former president Nixon for any crimes he may have committed. This meant Nixon could never be sent to jail for his involvement in the Watergate scandal.

RESPECTED STATESMAN

Nixon left the White House in disgrace. For the next 20 years, Nixon worked to win back America's respect. He wrote books on politics and world peace. Nixon also met with Presidents Ronald Reagan, George H.W. Bush, and Bill Clinton to give them advice.

On July 19, 1990, Nixon was honored at the grand opening of the Richard Nixon Library & Birthplace. It is located in Yorba Linda, California. Presidents George H.W. Bush, Ronald Reagan, and Gerald Ford also attended the celebration.

Pat Nixon died on June 22, 1993. Less than one year later, Richard Nixon died. He had a **stroke** on April 22, 1994, in New York City, New York. Nixon had just finished writing his eleventh book.

For many, the Watergate **scandal** and Nixon's resignation are his most lasting legacies. But as president, he helped improve the lives of Americans. He signed laws to protect the **environment** and to improve conditions for American workers. Richard Nixon worked to bring peace to the world.

Left to right: *Presidents Ronald Reagan, Richard Nixon, George H.W. Bush, and Gerald Ford at the Richard Nixon Library & Birthplace*

OFFICE OF THE PRESIDENT

BRANCHES OF GOVERNMENT

The U.S. government is divided into three branches. They are the executive, legislative, and judicial branches. This division is called a separation of powers. Each branch has some power over the others. This is called a system of checks and balances.

EXECUTIVE BRANCH

The executive branch enforces laws. It is made up of the president, the vice president, and the president's cabinet. The president represents the United States around the world. He or she oversees relations with other countries and signs treaties. The president signs bills into law and appoints officials and federal judges. He or she also leads the military and manages government workers.

LEGISLATIVE BRANCH

The legislative branch makes laws, maintains the military, and regulates trade. It also has the power to declare war. This branch consists of the Senate and the House of Representatives. Together, these two houses make up Congress. Each state has two senators. A state's population determines the number of representatives it has.

JUDICIAL BRANCH

The judicial branch interprets laws. It consists of district courts, courts of appeals, and the Supreme Court. District courts try cases. If a person disagrees with a trial's outcome, he or she may appeal. If the courts of appeals support the ruling, a person may appeal to the Supreme Court. The Supreme Court also makes sure that laws follow the U.S. Constitution.

QUALIFICATIONS FOR OFFICE

To be president, a person must meet three requirements. A candidate must be at least 35 years old and a natural-born U.S. citizen. He or she must also have lived in the United States for at least 14 years.

ELECTORAL COLLEGE

The U.S. presidential election is an indirect election. Voters from each state choose electors to represent them in the Electoral College. The number of electors from each state is based on population. Each elector has one electoral vote. Electors are pledged to cast their vote for the candidate who receives the highest number of popular votes in their state. A candidate must receive the majority of Electoral College votes to win.

TERM OF OFFICE

Each president may be elected to two four-year terms. Sometimes, a president may only be elected once. This happens if he or she served more than two years of the previous president's term.

The presidential election is held on the Tuesday after the first Monday in November. The president is sworn in on January 20 of the following year. At that time, he or she takes the oath of office:

I do solemnly swear (or affirm) that I will faithfully execute the office of President of the United States, and will to the best of my ability, preserve, protect and defend the Constitution of the United States.

LINE OF SUCCESSION

The Presidential Succession Act of 1947 defines who becomes president if the president cannot serve. The vice president is first in the line of succession. Next are the Speaker of the House and the President Pro Tempore of the Senate. If none of these individuals is able to serve, the office falls to the president's cabinet members. They would take office in the order in which each department was created:

Secretary of State

Secretary of the Treasury

Secretary of Defense

Attorney General

Secretary of the Interior

Secretary of Agriculture

Secretary of Commerce

Secretary of Labor

Secretary of Health and Human Services

Secretary of Housing and Urban Development

Secretary of Transportation

Secretary of Energy

Secretary of Education

Secretary of Veterans Affairs

Secretary of Homeland Security

BENEFITS

- While in office, the president receives a salary of $400,000 each year. He or she lives in the White House and has 24-hour Secret Service protection.

- The president may travel on a Boeing 747 jet called Air Force One. The airplane can accommodate 70 passengers. It has kitchens, a dining room, sleeping areas, and a conference room. It also has fully equipped offices with the latest communications systems. Air Force One can fly halfway around the world before needing to refuel. It can even refuel in flight!

- If the president wishes to travel by car, he or she uses Cadillac One. Cadillac One is a Cadillac Deville. It has been modified with heavy armor and communications systems. The president takes Cadillac One along when visiting other countries if secure transportation will be needed.

- The president also travels on a helicopter called Marine One. Like the presidential car, Marine One accompanies the president when traveling abroad if necessary.

- Sometimes, the president needs to get away and relax with family and friends. Camp David is the official presidential retreat. It is located in the cool, wooded mountains in Maryland. The U.S. Navy maintains the retreat, and the U.S. Marine Corps keeps it secure. The camp offers swimming, tennis, golf, and hiking.

- When the president leaves office, he or she receives Secret Service protection for ten more years. He or she also receives a yearly pension of $191,300 and funding for office space, supplies, and staff.

PRESIDENTS AND THEIR TERMS

PRESIDENT	PARTY	TOOK OFFICE	LEFT OFFICE	TERMS SERVED	VICE PRESIDENT
George Washington	None	April 30, 1789	March 4, 1797	Two	John Adams
John Adams	Federalist	March 4, 1797	March 4, 1801	One	Thomas Jefferson
Thomas Jefferson	Democratic-Republican	March 4, 1801	March 4, 1809	Two	Aaron Burr, George Clinton
James Madison	Democratic-Republican	March 4, 1809	March 4, 1817	Two	George Clinton, Elbridge Gerry
James Monroe	Democratic-Republican	March 4, 1817	March 4, 1825	Two	Daniel D. Tompkins
John Quincy Adams	Democratic-Republican	March 4, 1825	March 4, 1829	One	John C. Calhoun
Andrew Jackson	Democrat	March 4, 1829	March 4, 1837	Two	John C. Calhoun, Martin Van Buren
Martin Van Buren	Democrat	March 4, 1837	March 4, 1841	One	Richard M. Johnson
William H. Harrison	Whig	March 4, 1841	April 4, 1841	Died During First Term	John Tyler
John Tyler	Whig	April 6, 1841	March 4, 1845	Completed Harrison's Term	Office Vacant
James K. Polk	Democrat	March 4, 1845	March 4, 1849	One	George M. Dallas
Zachary Taylor	Whig	March 5, 1849	July 9, 1850	Died During First Term	Millard Fillmore

PRESIDENT	PARTY	TOOK OFFICE	LEFT OFFICE	TERMS SERVED	VICE PRESIDENT
Millard Fillmore	Whig	July 10, 1850	March 4, 1853	Completed Taylor's Term	Office Vacant
Franklin Pierce	Democrat	March 4, 1853	March 4, 1857	One	William R.D. King
James Buchanan	Democrat	March 4, 1857	March 4, 1861	One	John C. Breckinridge
Abraham Lincoln	Republican	March 4, 1861	April 15, 1865	Served One Term, Died During Second Term	Hannibal Hamlin, Andrew Johnson
Andrew Johnson	Democrat	April 15, 1865	March 4, 1869	Completed Lincoln's Second Term	Office Vacant
Ulysses S. Grant	Republican	March 4, 1869	March 4, 1877	Two	Schuyler Colfax, Henry Wilson
Rutherford B. Hayes	Republican	March 3, 1877	March 4, 1881	One	William A. Wheeler
James A. Garfield	Republican	March 4, 1881	September 19, 1881	Died During First Term	Chester Arthur
Chester Arthur	Republican	September 20, 1881	March 4, 1885	Completed Garfield's Term	Office Vacant
Grover Cleveland	Democrat	March 4, 1885	March 4, 1889	One	Thomas A. Hendricks
Benjamin Harrison	Republican	March 4, 1889	March 4, 1893	One	Levi P. Morton
Grover Cleveland	Democrat	March 4, 1893	March 4, 1897	One	Adlai E. Stevenson
William McKinley	Republican	March 4, 1897	September 14, 1901	Served One Term, Died During Second Term	Garret A. Hobart, Theodore Roosevelt

PRESIDENT	PARTY	TOOK OFFICE	LEFT OFFICE	TERMS SERVED	VICE PRESIDENT
Theodore Roosevelt	Republican	September 14, 1901	March 4, 1909	Completed McKinley's Second Term, Served One Term	Office Vacant, Charles Fairbanks
William Taft	Republican	March 4, 1909	March 4, 1913	One	James S. Sherman
Woodrow Wilson	Democrat	March 4, 1913	March 4, 1921	Two	Thomas R. Marshall
Warren G. Harding	Republican	March 4, 1921	August 2, 1923	Died During First Term	Calvin Coolidge
Calvin Coolidge	Republican	August 3, 1923	March 4, 1929	Completed Harding's Term, Served One Term	Office Vacant, Charles Dawes
Herbert Hoover	Republican	March 4, 1929	March 4, 1933	One	Charles Curtis
Franklin D. Roosevelt	Democrat	March 4, 1933	April 12, 1945	Served Three Terms, Died During Fourth Term	John Nance Garner, Henry A. Wallace, Harry S. Truman
Harry S. Truman	Democrat	April 12, 1945	January 20, 1953	Completed Roosevelt's Fourth Term, Served One Term	Office Vacant, Alben Barkley
Dwight D. Eisenhower	Republican	January 20, 1953	January 20, 1961	Two	Richard Nixon
John F. Kennedy	Democrat	January 20, 1961	November 22, 1963	Died During First Term	Lyndon B. Johnson
Lyndon B. Johnson	Democrat	November 22, 1963	January 20, 1969	Completed Kennedy's Term, Served One Term	Office Vacant, Hubert H. Humphrey
Richard Nixon	Republican	January 20, 1969	August 9, 1974	Completed First Term, Resigned During Second Term	Spiro T. Agnew, Gerald Ford

PRESIDENT	PARTY	TOOK OFFICE	LEFT OFFICE	TERMS SERVED	VICE PRESIDENT
Gerald Ford	Republican	August 9, 1974	January 20, 1977	Completed Nixon's Second Term	Nelson A. Rockefeller
Jimmy Carter	Democrat	January 20, 1977	January 20, 1981	One	Walter Mondale
Ronald Reagan	Republican	January 20, 1981	January 20, 1989	Two	George H.W. Bush
George H.W. Bush	Republican	January 20, 1989	January 20, 1993	One	Dan Quayle
Bill Clinton	Democrat	January 20, 1993	January 20, 2001	Two	Al Gore
George W. Bush	Republican	January 20, 2001	January 20, 2009	Two	Dick Cheney
Barack Obama	Democrat	January 20, 2009			Joe Biden

"I have often said, what is really important in a person's life is whether they make a difference, a difference for the benefit of others."
Richard Nixon

WRITE TO THE PRESIDENT

You may write to the president at:

**The White House
1600 Pennsylvania Avenue NW
Washington, DC 20500**

You may e-mail the president at:
comments@whitehouse.gov

GLOSSARY

ballot - a piece of paper used to cast a vote.

bar association - an organization of individuals who are qualified to practice law.

cabinet - a group of advisers chosen by the president to lead government departments.

Cold War - a period of tension and hostility between the United States and its allies and the Soviet Union and its allies after World War II.

debate - a contest in which two sides argue for or against something.

Democrat - a member of the Democratic political party. Democrats believe in social change and strong government.

Democratic National Committee - a group that provides leadership for the Democratic Party.

environment - all the surroundings that affect the growth and well-being of a living thing.

impeach - to charge a public official with misconduct in office.

inaugurate (ih-NAW-gyuh-rayt) - to swear into a political office.

incumbent - the current holder of an office.

inflation - a rise in the price of goods and services.

Marshall Plan - a program that gave economic and technical assistance to 16 European countries to help them rebuild after World War II.

partner - an owner in a business, such as a law firm. Partners share the money the business makes, as well as its losses.

perjury - telling a lie when under oath to tell the truth.

popular vote - the vote of the entire body of people with the right to vote.

Quaker - a member of the religious group called the Society of Friends.

Republican - a member of the Republican political party. Republicans are conservative and believe in small government.

Republican National Committee - a group that provides leadership for the Republican Party.

running mate - a candidate running for a lower-rank position on an election ticket, especially the candidate for vice president.

scandal - an action that shocks people and disgraces those connected with it.

scholarship - a gift of money to help a student pay for instruction.

Six-Day War - from June 5 to June 10, 1967. A war fought between Israel, Egypt, Jordan, and Syria.

stroke - a sudden loss of consciousness, sensation, and voluntary motion. This attack of paralysis is caused by a rupture to a blood vessel of the brain, often caused by a blood clot.

Taft-Hartley Act - a law that restricted the activities of labor unions.

tuberculosis - a disease that affects the lungs.

Vietnam War - from 1957 to 1975. A long, failed attempt by the United States to stop North Vietnam from taking over South Vietnam.

World War II - from 1939 to 1945, fought in Europe, Asia, and Africa. Great Britain, France, the United States, the Soviet Union, and their allies were on one side. Germany, Italy, Japan, and their allies were on the other side.

WEB SITES

To learn more about Richard Nixon, visit ABDO Publishing Company on the World Wide Web at **www.abdopublishing.com**. Web sites about Richard Nixon are featured on our Book Links page. These links are routinely monitored and updated to provide the most current information available.

INDEX